M. Glenys Cosy

The Divine Compassion

A Cantata
for Tenor and Baritone Soloists, Chorus and Organ

WILLIAM LLOYD WEBBER

Kevin
Mayhew

We hope you enjoy the music in this book. Further copies are available from your local music shop or Christian bookshop.

In case of difficulty, please contact the publisher direct by writing to:

The Sales Department
KEVIN MAYHEW LTD
Buxhall
Stowmarket
Suffolk
IP14 3BW

Phone 01449 737978
Fax 01449 737834

Please ask for our complete catalogue of outstanding Church Music.

First published in Great Britain in 1996 by Kevin Mayhew Ltd.

ISBN 0 86209 872 6
Catalogue No: 1450051

0 1 2 3 4 5 6 7 8 9

Front Cover: *Let he who is without sin cast the first stone*
by Sebastiano Conca (*c*.1676-1764)).
Courtesy of Rafael Valls Gallery. Reproduced by kind permission.
Cover design by Veronica Ward and Graham Johnstone.

Music Editor: Donald Thomson
Music setting by Tracy Cracknell

Printed and bound in Great Britain

Contents

About the Composer

'One of the finest all-round musicians Britain has produced this century'. This is how Bryan Hesford of *Musical Opinion* described William Lloyd Webber at the time of his death in 1982. Besides leading a distinguished career in London's academic institutions (Director of the London College of Music, Professor at the Royal College of Music) and winning renown as a brilliant organist, William Lloyd Webber also composed music in many different spheres. Highly romantic in style, it shows the influence of Franck, Sibelius and Rachmaninov. Of his orchestral tone poem *Aurora* recorded by Lorin Maazel and the London Philharmonic Orchestra (Philips 420 342-2), Edward Greenfield wrote in *The Guardian,* 'skilfully and sumptuously scored, it is music as sensuous as any you will find from a British composer,' and of his *Missa Sanctae Mariae Magdalenae* Geoffrey Norris wrote in *The Daily Telegraph,* 'Beautiful deeply felt writing – an instinctive feeling for words and choral colouring – a striking impressive force.' This Mass, together with some of the songs, piano works and chamber music, is available on an ASV CD (DCA961).

Other music by William Lloyd Webber published by Kevin Mayhew Ltd. includes:

	Catalogue No
Piano music	
Six Pieces for Piano	3611148
Scenes from Childhood - seven pieces for piano	3611171
Three Pieces for Piano	3611196
Organ music	
Aria – thirteen pieces for organ	1400028
Chorale, Cantilena and Finale	1400073
Reflections – seven pieces for organ	1400083
Choral and vocal music	
Born a King – A Christmas Cantata	1400007
Missa Sanctae Mariae Magdalenae	1450060
The Songs of William Lloyd Webber	3611169

THE DIVINE COMPASSION

Text: Selected from the Gospel of John by Albert F Bayly (1901-1984)
Music: William Lloyd Webber (1914-1982)

PART I

THE GLORY INCARNATE

the glo - ry as of the on - ly be - got - ten of the Fa - ther full of grace and truth.

Moderato, ma con moto (♩ = 100)

Full *ff*

S: O glo - ry of the word of God e - ter - nal, shin - ing be-fore the

A: O glo - ry of the word of God e - ter - nal, be - fore the

T: O glo - ry of the word of God e - ter - nal, shin - ing be-fore the

B: O glo - ry of the word of God e - ter - nal, be - fore the

an - cient stars were born: glo - ry most ex - cel -lent of ve - ry

stars were born: glo - ry, glo - ry of ve - ry

stars were born: glo - ry most ex - cel - lent of ve - ry

an - cient stars were born: glo - ry, glo - ry of ve - ry

God - head, life - giv - ing ra - diance of in - fi - ni - ty, of in -

God - head, life - giv - ing ra - diance of in - fi - ni - ty, of in -

God - head, life - giv - ing ra - diance of in - fi - ni - ty, ra - diance of in -

God - head, life - giv - ing ra - diance of in - fi - ni - ty, in -

Don't turn here

9

earth, be lif – ted up from the earth, will draw all men un – to me.

si – lent – ly the grain u – pon the soil; dies

Evangelist

Falls

to a so-li-ta-ry life, but bears a har-vest rich, a har-vest rich to fill, to fill out hu-man need. So dies God's grain of wheat, the Son of Man; hid-den in earth's dark soil to

cresc.

cresc.

f

f

Poco meno mosso

p

mp

p

pp

pp

Ped.

sleep,   to sleep   en - tombed,   but

glo - rious,   glo - rious that tomb,   for thence up-springs a

life   to   feed the hun - gry   mul - ti - tude,   but

glo - rious that   tomb,   for thence up - springs a   life,   for

13

thence up-springs a life, a life, a life to feed the

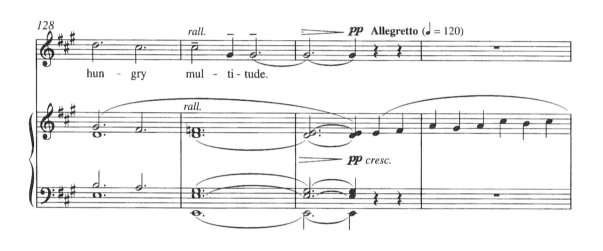

hun - gry mul - ti - tude.

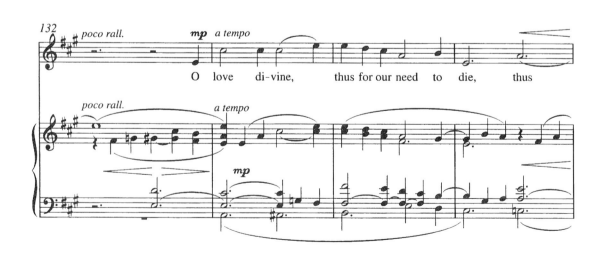

O love di-vine, thus for our need to die, thus

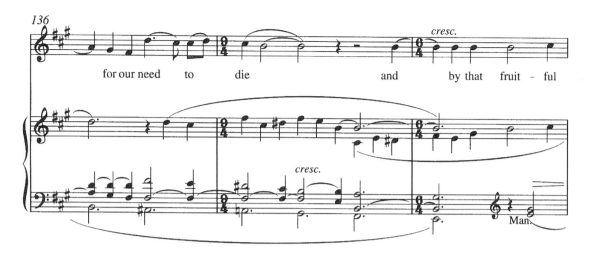

for our need to die and by that fruit - ful

death, by that death our life sup - ply, by that

death our life sup - ply. O love di - vine, O

15

love di-vine, love di - vine, O love, O

love di - vine.

CHRIST, THE BREAD OF LIFE

CHRIST, THE GOOD SHEPHERD

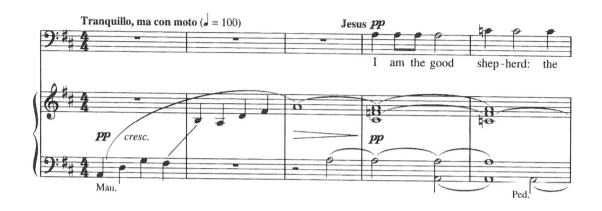

and I lay down my life for the sheep.   And

o-ther sheep I have which are not of this fold: them al-so

must I bring, and they shall hear my voice: and there shall be one flock,

and one shep - herd.

ADORATION OF CHRIST, THE FAITHFUL SHEPHERD

heed-ed,   yet hast thou brought the suc-cour that we need-ed, though   Sav - iour,

all   it   cost thee,   though Sav - iour, all   it   cost thee.

though   Sav - iour,   Sav-iour, all   it   cost thee.

Poco a poco in tempo I

Then   must   thy sheep,   O

Then   must   thy sheep,   O

Poco a poco in tempo I

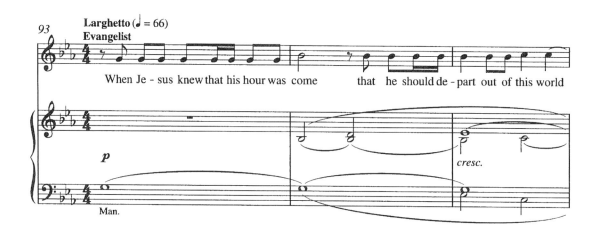

THE LOVE OF CHRIST

THE HIGH-PRIESTLY INTERCESSION

that they may be one, e - ven as we are one:

Tranquillo (♩ = 84)

I in them, and thou in me, that

they may be made per - fect in one; and that the world may

know that thou hast sent me, and hast loved them

them, and I in them, that the love may be in them, may

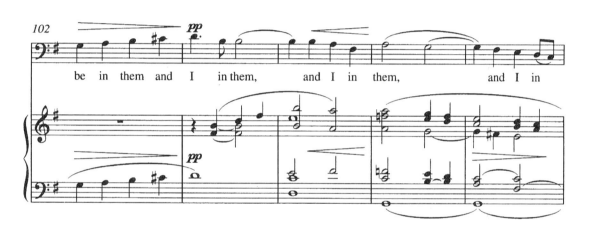

be in them and I in them, and I in them, and I in

them, I in them.

THE CHRISTIAN SOUL'S RESPONSE TO CHRIST'S PRAYER

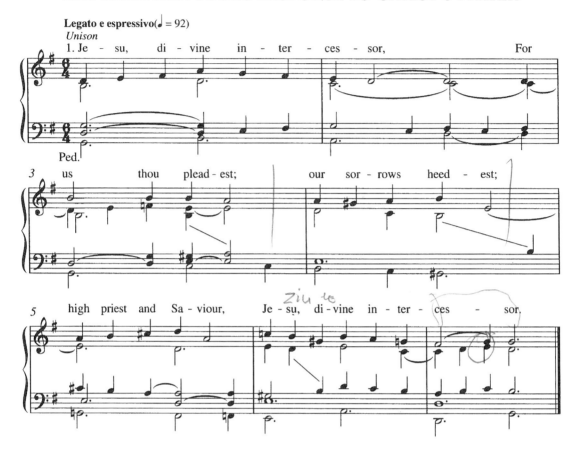

2. Jesu, divine intercessor,
   in thy prayer spoken,
   in thy heart broken,
   shines God's compassion,
   Jesu, divine intercessor.

3. Jesu, divine intercessor,
   thine all thou gavest,
   and now thou savest
   us who receive thee
   Jesu, divine intercessor.

4. Jesu, divine intercessor,
   join us in union,
   one blest communion,
   thou in us dwelling;
   Jesu, divine intercessor.

5. Jesu, divine intercessor,
   let our life show thee,
   that all may know thee,
   sent by the Father,
   Jesu, divine intercessor.

Text: Albert F Bayly (1901-1984)

PART II

THE GLORY OF SACRIFICE

Larghetto (♩ = 63)

Evangelist *p*

When Je - sus had spo - ken these words, he went forth with his dis -

Man.

ci - ples o - ver the brook Ce - dron, where was a gar - den.

And Ju - das al - so, which be - trayed him, knew the place.

attacca

CHRIST BETRAYED

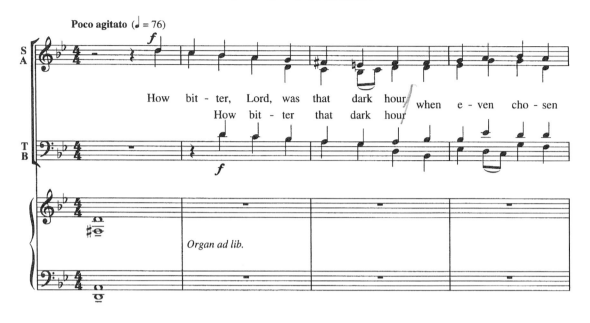

How bit - ter, Lord, was that dark hour when e - ven cho - sen
How bit - ter that dark hour

Organ ad lib.

friend be - trayed: when all the weight of e - vil's pow'r u - pon thy

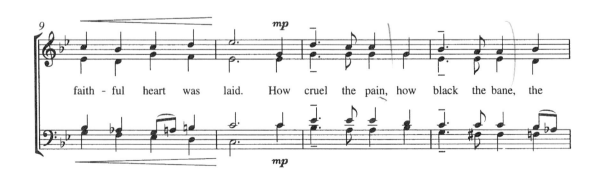

faith - ful heart was laid. How cruel the pain, how black the bane, the

poi - son of that cup by Sa - tan made. More bit - ter still, I
More bit - ter

tell with shame that I for whom thou bar - est all have scorned thy
still, I tell that I

love, be-trayed thy name, and shared the trai - tor Ju - das' fall. Can'st thou for-give, and

let me live, who pe - ni - tent doth on thy mer - cy call?

THE ARREST

CHRIST IN THE HANDS OF HIS ENEMIES

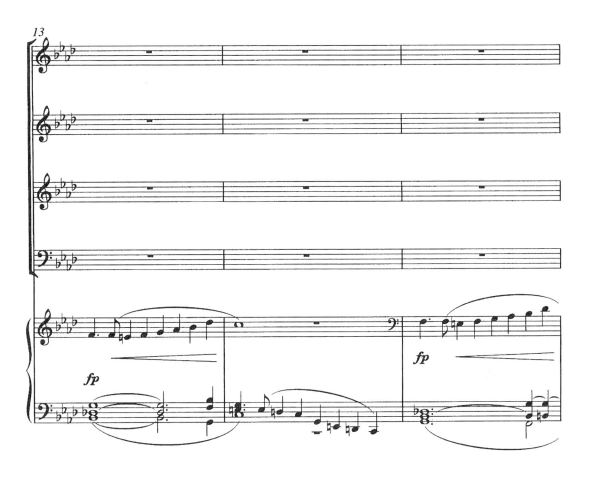

Here in de-feat and shame we see God's glo - ry.

Here in de-feat and shame we see God's glo - ry.

Here in o-be-dience his tri-um-phant might. Here faith-ful love and

Here in o-be-dience his tri-um-phant might. Here faith-ful love and

Christ goes to con - quer, to

Christ goes to con - quer, to

suff'-ring tell the sto - ry, Christ goes to con - quer,

suff'-ring tell the sto - ry, Christ goes to con - quer,

PETER'S DENIAL OF CHRIST

see thee in the gar - den with him?

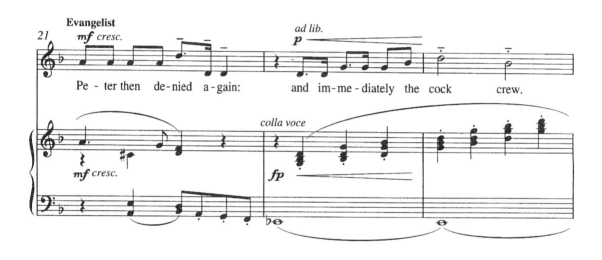

Evangelist

Pe - ter then de - nied a - gain: and im - me - diately the cock crew.

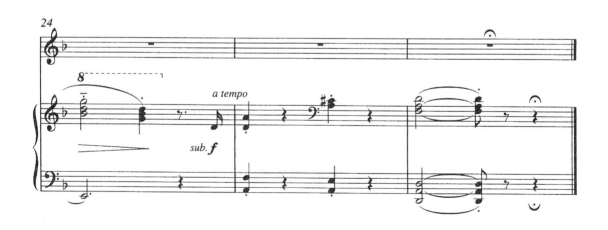

CHRIST DENIED BY HIS FRIEND

base - ly I de - nied. O weak heart, well I know thee! Mine

too has been thy sin. O Christ, de-nied, for -

O Christ, de - nied, for - sa - ken; O

O Christ, de - nied, for - sa - ken; O

O Christ, de - nied, O

O Christ, de - nied, O

Allegro marziale (♩ = 120)

Man.

Evangelist *mf marcato*

Now An - nas had sent him bound un - to

Cai - a - phas the high priest. Then led they Je - sus

un - to the hall of judge - ment. Pi - late then went out un - to them and said:

that is of the truth hear - eth my voice.

Man.

molto rall.

Pilate *p* *fp*

What is truth?

pp

molto rall.

fp

Man.

Subito allegro marziale (♩ = 120)

Evangelist *f marcato*

And when he had

pp cresc.

f

Ped.

fmp

said this, he went out a - gain un-to the Jews, and said un - to

fmp

cresc.

Man.

this man, but Ba-rab-bas! Not this man, but Ba-rab-bas! Not this man,

Evangelist

Now Ba - ra - bas

but Ba-rab - bas!

was a rob - ber.

Man.

attacca

CHRIST JUDGED BY WORLDLY POWER

Art thou a king?

e-ter-nal glo - ry shall sur-round, shall sur-round thy

head.

S Thou art the king, O Christ, of love and truth. Thine age-less king-dom shall en-

A Thou art the king of love and truth Thine age-less king-dom shall en-

T Thou art the king, O Christ, of love and truth. Thine age-less king - dom

B Thou art the king of truth. Thine age - less king - dom,

CHRIST MOCKED AND CONDEMNED

Then Pi - late there - fore took Je - sus, and

scour - ged him. And the sol - diers plai - ted a crown of thorns, and

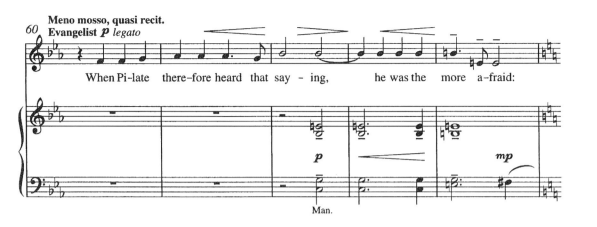

Meno mosso, quasi recit.
Evangelist *p legato*

When Pi-late there-fore heard that say - ing, he was the more a-fraid:

Man.

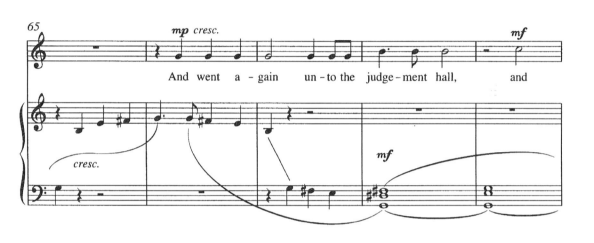

And went a - gain un - to the judge-ment hall, and

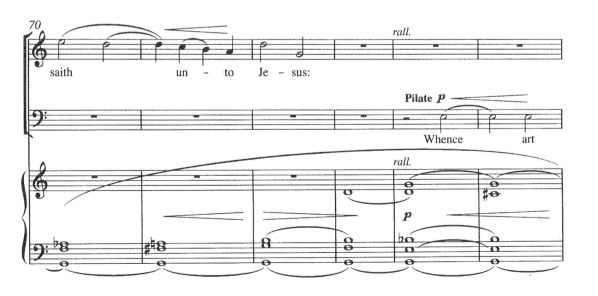

saith un - to Je - sus:

Pilate *p*

Whence art

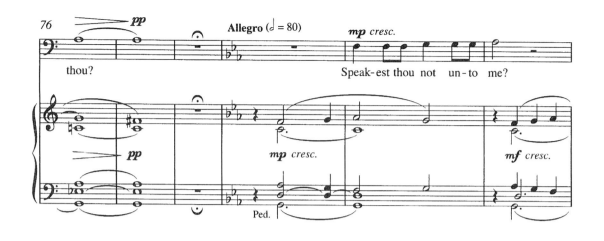

76

thou? Speak-est thou not un-to me?

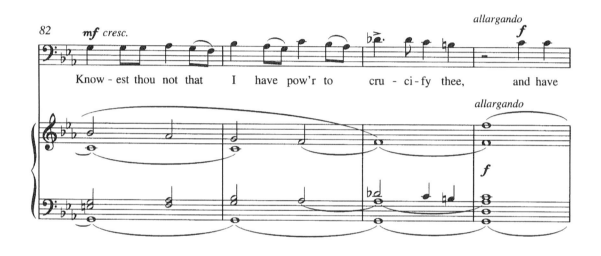

82

Know - est thou not that I have pow'r to cru - ci - fy thee, and have

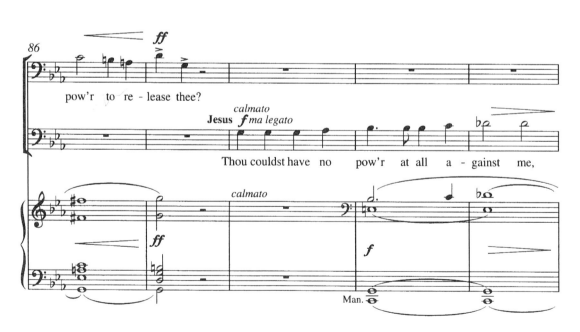

86

pow'r to re - lease thee?

Jesus

Thou couldst have no pow'r at all a - gainst me,

ex-cept it were gi - ven thee from a - bove:

there - fore

Man.

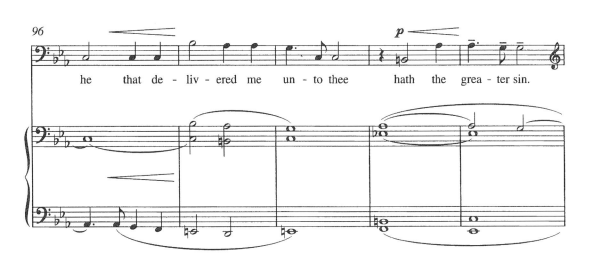

he that de - liv - ered me un - to thee hath the grea - ter sin.

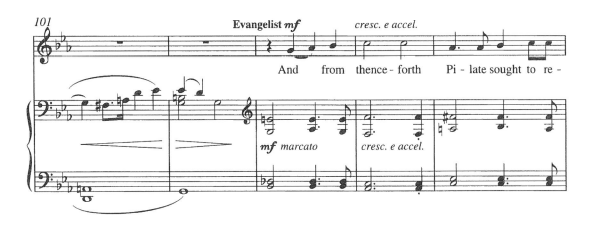

Evangelist *mf* *cresc. e accel.*

And from thence - forth Pi - late sought to re -

mf marcato *cresc. e accel.*

Who - so - e - ver ma - keth him - self a king speak -

Man.

- eth, speak - eth a - gainst Cae - sar.

Allegro marziale($\\quad$ = 120)

Evangelist *p cresc. e accel. poco a poco*

When Pi - late there - fore heard that

accel. poco a poco

pp cresc. poco a poco

Ped.

THE CONDEMNATION OF CHRIST

CHRIST CRUCIFIED

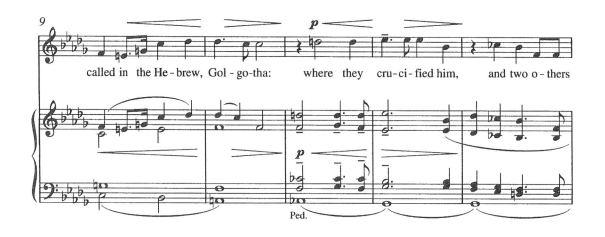

called in the He - brew, Gol - go - tha: where they cru - ci - fied him, and two o - thers

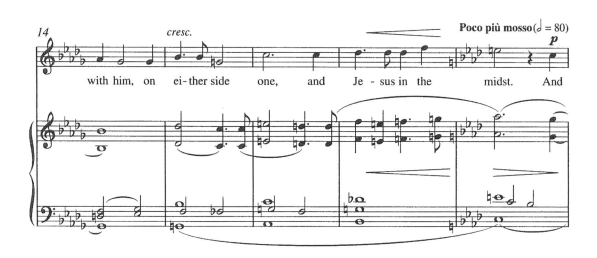

with him, on ei - ther side one, and Je - sus in the midst. And

Pi - late wrote a ti - tle, and put it on the cross, and the

- ven from the top through-out. They said there-fore:

Chorus of Soldiers

Let us not rend it, but cast lots for it, whose it shall be.

Evangelist

Now there stood by the cross of Je - sus his

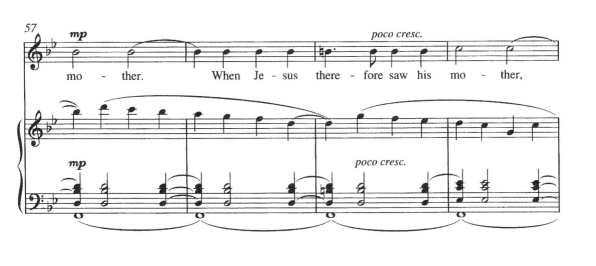

mo - ther. When Je - sus there - fore saw his mo - ther,

and the dis - ci - ple stand - ing by, whom he loved, he

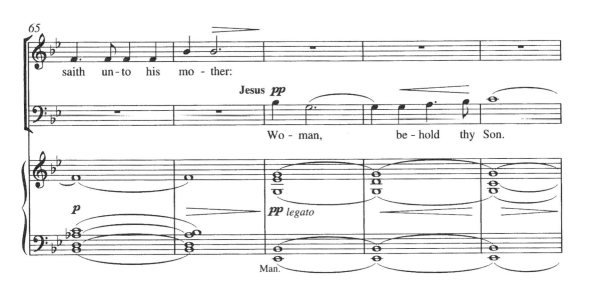

saith un - to his mo - ther:

Jesus *pp* Wo - man, be - hold thy Son.

Man.

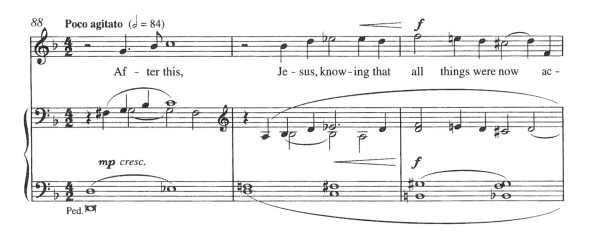

Poco agitato (♩ = 84)

Af - ter this, Je - sus, know-ing that all things were now ac -

com-plished, that the script-tures might be ful - filled, saith:

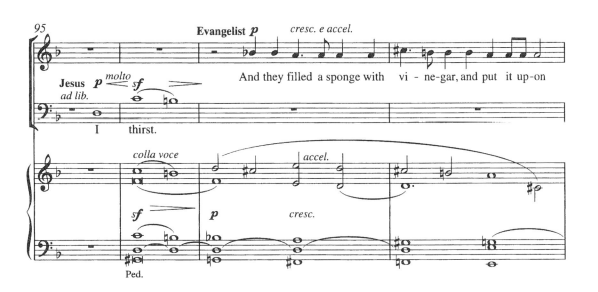

Jesus: I thirst.

Evangelist: And they filled a sponge with vi - ne-gar, and put it up-on

Congregational Hymn

THE GLORY OF THE CRUCIFIED

1. Was there no glo-ry in that hour when on the cross our Sa - viour died? When all the force of Sa - tan's pow'r was hurled a - gainst the cru - ci - fied?

2. Was there no glory when his head
was bowed in death's last agony?
no glory when his body bled
with cruel nails fixed on the tree?

3. Yes, there was glory, brighter far
than crowns the head of earthly king;
a glory time shall never mar,
and hearts adoring ever sing.

4. There shone the glory of a love
which neither sin nor death could break,
divine compassion from above,
in dying word and action spake.

5. Glory of God's own sacrifice,
which, giving all, won for our race,
by that immeasurable price,
in his eternal realm, a place.

6. Glory of Jesus crucified,
we bow before thy burning ray;
with shame confess our sinful pride,
and humbly for thy mercy pray.

7. Then may that glory light our life;
our praise inspire, our love constrain
and nerve us for the spirit's strife
till Christ within us fully reign.

Text: Albert F Bayly (1901-1984)
Text © Copyright Oxford University Press. Used by permission.

PART III

THE RESURRECTION GLORY

li - nen clothes with the spi - ces.

Now in the place where he was cru - ci - fied there was a gar - den:

and in that gar-den a new se - pul-chre, where-in was ne - ver man yet laid:

Meno mosso e espress.

There laid they Je - sus.

CHRIST IN THE TOMB

ci - ple, and came to the se - pul - chre. And the o - ther dis-

ci - ple did out - run Pe - ter, and came first to the se - pul - chre.

And he, stoop - ing down, and look - ing in, saw the

li - nen clothes lie. And the nap - kin that was a - bout his

head wrapped to-ge – ther in a place by it-self.

Man.

Ped.

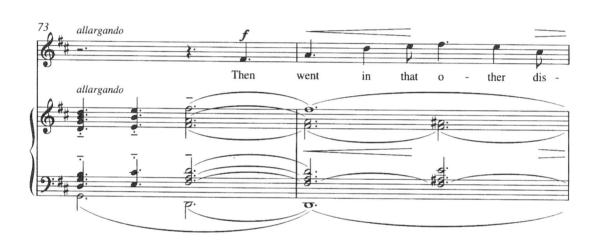

allargando

allargando

Then went in that o – ther dis-

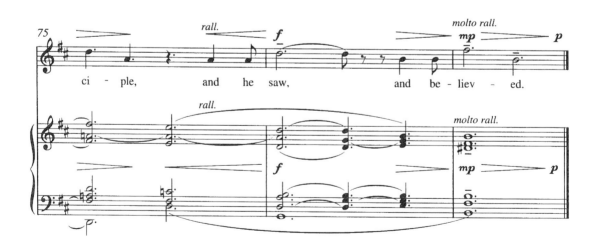

ci – ple, and he saw, and be – liev – ed.

THE DAWN OF HOPE

parts,   life's dawn re - joi - ces,   re - joi - ces grief - sha - dowed hearts.

parts,   life's dawn re - joi - ces,   re - joi - ces grief - sha - dowed hearts.

parts,   life's dawn re - joi - ces,   re - joi - ces grief - sha - dowed hearts.

parts,   dawn   re - joi - ces,   re - joi - ces grief - sha - dowed hearts.

Then the dis - ci - ples went a - way a - gain   un - to their own

home.   But Ma - ry stood with - out   at the se - pul - chre, weep - ing: and as she

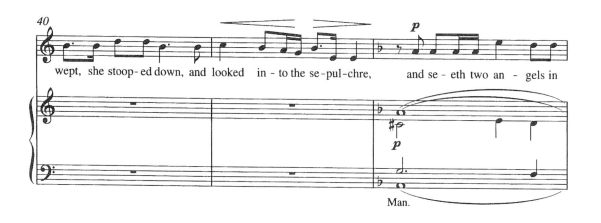

wept, she stoop-ed down, and looked in - to the se -pul-chre, and se - eth two an - gels in

Man.

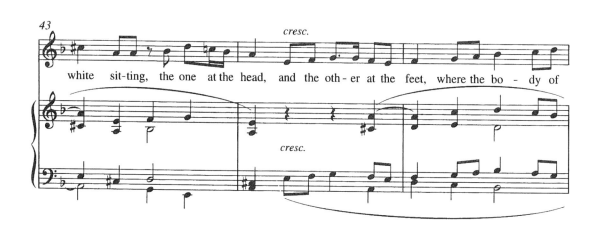

white sit-ting, the one at the head, and the oth - er at the feet, where the bo - dy of

Je - sus had lain. And they say un-to her:

Angels (S & A Duet or Semi-Chorus) *mp*

Wo - man, why

Ped.

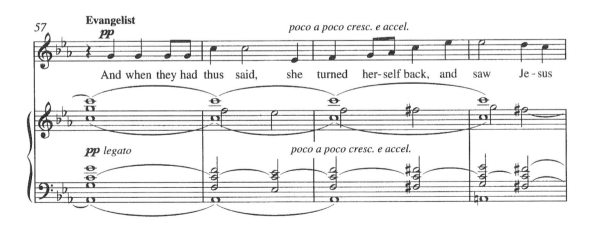

standing, and knew not that it was Jesus.

Jesus

Man.

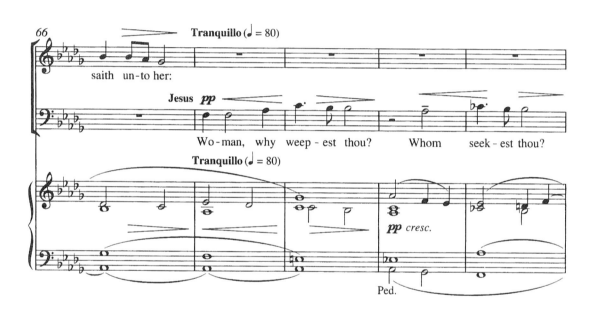

saith unto her:

Woman, why weepest thou? Whom seekest thou?

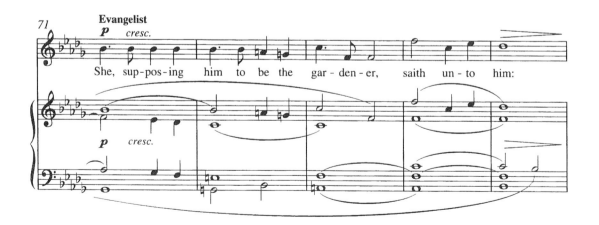

She, supposing him to be the gardener, saith unto him:

Jesus

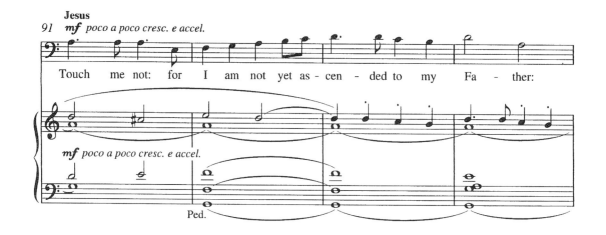

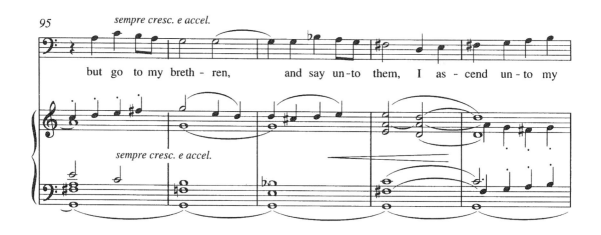

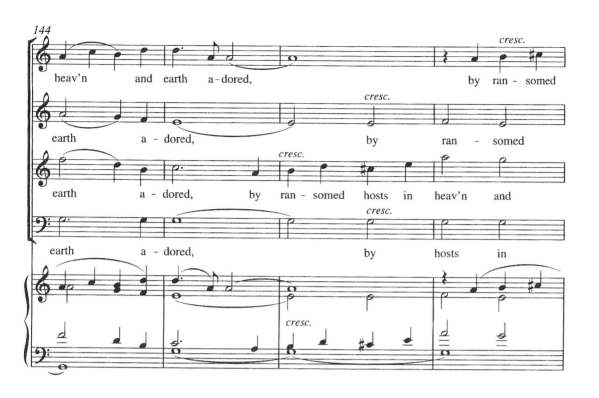

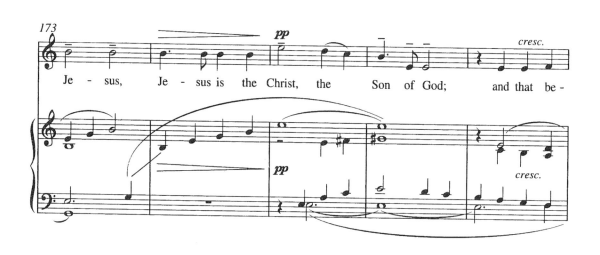

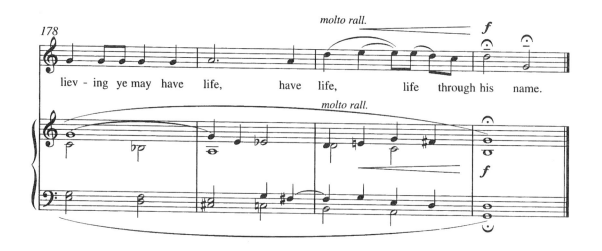